CONTENTS

Ahoy there, m'hearties! Do you know why some pirates wear purple braces with pink spots on them? And while you're thinking of the answer, let me introduce myself. 'Tis I, Captain Ben Blunder, the pirate who put the swash in swashbuckling and the buckle on his belt. Me and the rest of the crew of the good ship *Mad Maggot* are here to share some of our favourite jokes with you, such as –

What do you call a pirate with a seagull on his head?

Cliff!

Coming along on the trip is that black-hearted villain Captain Bill Sharkie and the crew of the *Vulture* who seem to think that the jokes they have to tell are funnier than mine – well, we'll see about that, Bill Sharkie. My wit is sharper than a buccaneer's blade!

Hot on our tails is *H.M.S. Hornet*, its hold full of underwear.

Why underwear, I hear you ask?

Because Roger Jolly wants to put us all under a vest!

We've given the best jokes a 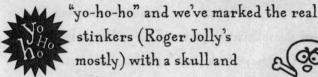 "yo-ho-ho" and we've marked the real stinkers (Roger Jolly's mostly) with a skull and crossbones.

So, up anchor, Ned Snuff. Raise the skull and crossbones, Betty Bilge, and let's set sail.

What was that you said?

Oh, you want to know why some pirates wear purple braces with pink spots on them.

To keep their trousers up of course!

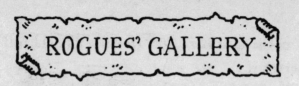

ROGUES' GALLERY

'Cap'n Blunder!' I hears a voice behind me.

'What is it, Dan?' I says.

''Ere we smuddock the spinnaker and grindle the genoa, don't 'e think thine reader people would like to know something about us?' says Dirty Dan.

'What is there to know?' I asks.

'Who we's all be,' replies Dan.

'Oh, I suppose so,' I says. 'How about if I take the readers into the Mess – '

'Not Ned Snuff's cabin?' says Dan.

'No. The Mess. Where we eat whatever Sam's sweated over – '

    'And into!'

'He does say he puts a lot of himself into his cooking,' I says. 'So how about if I take the readers into the Mess and show them the sketches the talented Mr Hawkins drew of us all.'

''Twill do better than a pair of binoculars to a one-eyed pirate,' says Dan.

'Right then,' I says. 'Let's get going.'

* * * * *

First and most important of all, 'tis I, Captain Ben Blunder, sometimes called 'Lucky' Ben Blunder. I didn't set out to be a pirate. I went for a day trip to France, got on the wrong boat, found myself cabin boy on a pirate vessel and

Captain Ben Blunder

I've been sailing the three seas ever since. What's that? You mean there are more than three seas?

Sweaty Sam

And this is Sweaty Sam – the *Mad Maggot*'s cook. Sam's meals are to cooking what pirates are to honest seafarers: something to be avoided as often as possible.

Betty Bilge

This buxom beauty is Betty Bilge, a pirate gel whose weakness for gems once led her to try to open a jewellery shop, but the alarm was raised before she got inside!

And here's Cutlass Kate, who I'm told has designs on me, but I don't fancy the idea of being tattooed... She was found abandoned in a sea chest by a fisherman called Kipper (a queer old fish if ever there was one).

Cutlass Kate

Ned Snuff

This likely-looking lad is Ned Snuff, who sometimes gets right up my nose. As a boy, Ned was a nimble-fingered pickpocket who was quick to learn that every crowd has a silver lining.

Dirty Dan

Here's my bosun, Dirty Dan, an old salt washed more in the lore of the sea than in the *Mad Maggot's* monthly bath.

That's Polly, my parrot. He's handy to have around when the *Mad Maggot* springs a leak, as he makes great Pollyfilla!

Polly

Rover

And this is Rover, my dog, loyal, intelligent – everything a pirate could ask for in a dog. Well, apart from the fact that he's petrified of cats – and eats like a hungry horse.

This black-hearted seadog is Beastly Bill Sharkie, captain of the *Vulture*, a ship as mean and sleek as Beastly Bill Sharkie himself.

Beastly Bill

Motley

Meet Motley, Beastly Bill Sharkie's mean-tempered cat. An animal with the milk of parrot-hatred flowing through his veins. This is the animal who put the cat into catapult.

Nasty Norman is one of Beastly Bill Sharkie's crew. To say he's shifty isn't so much stating the obvious as shouting it from the crow's nest.

Nasty Norman

Roger Jolly

Last is Commander Roger Jolly with his pet seagull, Sydney. Roger would be Roger Very Jolly if he could capture me and Beastly Bill Sharkie, but he's got more chance of clapping his hands at a pantomime than of clapping us two in irons!

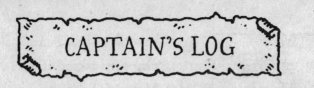

CAPTAIN'S LOG

A month aboard the *Mad Maggot*

1st May

Upped anchor and set sail for the Spanish Minor, that's like the Spanish Main but it's not so large! We'd just left port when Ned Snuff shouted down from the Crow's Nest, 'Man trying to board the Mad Maggot.'

'Who is it?' I cried.

'Francis Drake and his drum,' replied Ned.

'Well tell him to beat it!'

2nd May

Sailing along the coast I spotted a curious craft trying to catch up with us.

'Tis a woman paddling a pram,' called Betty Bilge, looking up from polishing her pearls.

'Tell her to push off,' I ordered.

3rd May

Received signal from passing ship asking if it's possible to hire the *Mad Maggot* for the day.

'Hire the *Mad Maggot* for the day?' I spluttered. 'What do they want us to do? Put a brick under her?'

4th May

To pass the time I organised a poetry competition which I won, of course, with the following:

I'm very good friends with a pelican
Who holds more in its mouth than its belly can.
It can store in its beak
What it eats in a week.
But I really don't know how the heck it can!

5th May

Heard a nasty rumour about an empty pirate galleon – but there was nothing in it.

6th May

Today I heard about a pirate who lives at the bottom of the sea – he's called Billy the Squid!

7th May

Overheard Betty Bilge
gossiping with Cutlass
Kate about the pirates
who stole a cargo of
soap from a merchant – they made a clean getaway!

8th May

Decided that the crew's geography was a bit ropy so
got the globe down from the shelf and called
everyone onto the poopdeck. 'Kate,' I said, handing
her a pointer. 'Where's Australia?'

Kate spun the globe, stopped it when Australia
came into view and put the end of the pointer on it.
'That's it there, Cap'n,' she said.

'Well done, Kate,' I said. 'Now, can anyone tell
me who discovered Australia?'

Sam's hand went up.

'Cutlass Kate!' he said, with a smirk on his face.

9th May

Betty Bilge reported on sick parade complaining she
had swallowed some gunpowder.

Ordered crew to ensure that Betty Bilge was not
to be pointed at me at all costs.

10th May

Found this piece of graffiti scrawled on deck –

A crusty old salt is Ben Blunder,
He takes passing ships for their plunder.
One day in Port Said,
He sat down and cried,
And sobbed, 'It's the strain that I'm under.'

Ordered Ned Snuff to wash it off.

11th May

Cancelled plans for a musical evening, as someone had stolen the loot!

12th May

Ordered Ned Snuff to clean my quarters as heard him talking about the Captain's Mess.

13th May

Dirty Dan asked why he felt he was going round in circles all the time.

Ordered him to keep quiet or I would lash his other foot to the mizzenmast!

14th May

Betty Bilge asked me what the difference is between a pirate and a bargain hunter.

Apparently, one goes to sail the sea and the other goes to see the sales.

From the way she laughed, at least one of us thought it was funny...

15th May

Found a fly in my soup at dinner today.

Ned Snuff said it had committed insecticide.

(Note: let Ned Snuff out of his chains at midnight.)

16th May

Saw a flock of geese overhead; wondered why birds fly south for winter.

Ned Snuff said because it was too far for them to walk.

(Note: put Ned Snuff back in chains tomorrow after he's scrubbed the deck – with a toothbrush.)

17th May

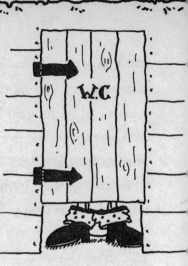

Crew wondered why I was so irritated when Dirty Dan locked himself in the lavatory for hours and I couldn't use it.

Don't they know that without a 'p' any pirate becomes irate!

18th May

Told crew that I'd like to get a new parrot for the *Mad Maggot*.

Sweaty Sam said that pet shops don't do swaps.

19th May

Saw *HMS Hornet* on the horizon and got a bad attack of hiccups.

Betty Bilge suggested I draw alongside and ask Commander Jolly for a pardon.

(Note: suggest it's time Betty Bilge found a ship of her own!)

20th May

Ned Snuff spotted an Egyptian pirate ship flying the 'sickness aboard' flag; turned out all the crew have come down with flu. They caught it from their mummies!

21st May

Must report spooky experience. Sailed alongside a ship, and the crew reported it was deserted. Then Dirty Dan shouted, 'It's the Invisible Man's ship, Sir. He wants to come on board.'

I shouted back, 'Tell him I can't see him.'

22nd May

Boarded a Spanish treasure galleon and took much booty aboard. 'Cap'n,' said Dirty Dan. 'Now we've got this loot, what will we do with the begging letters?'

Thought for a moment then said, 'Oh, keep on sending them, Dan.'

23rd May

'Cap'n,' shouted Ned Snuff. 'There's a long white line stretching across the sea as far as I can see.'

'I'm not surprised,' I shouted back. 'When I was on watch we were passed by an ocean liner.'

24th May

At dinner today, Cutlass Kate told us of the day a
ship she was on was overturned by a tidal wave.

'What happened?' asked Ned Snuff.

'I was washed up on a beach where a dance was
being held,' she replied.

'A dance?' we all said at the same time.

'Yes!' Kate laughed. 'It was a beach ball!'

25th May

Noticed Ned Snuff squinting through his telescope.
'Have your eyes ever been checked, Ned?' I asked.

'No, Cap'n!' he replied. 'They've always been
blue.'

26th May

Ned Snuff reported seeing a huge prehistoric animal rising from the waves.

Probably a Tyrannosaurus Wreck!

27th May

Decided to try my hand at a few conjuring tricks to keep the crew amused, but after each trick Poll squawked, 'I know how you did it! I know how you did it!' Became so annoyed that I devised a spectacular trick that Poll would find impossible to get to the bottom of. But when I was halfway through it, down in the galley, Sweaty Sam dropped a match into a can of oil and with a blinding flash and a mighty explosion, the *Mad Maggot* sank, but not before we had scrambled for the lifeboat and rowed to safety.

We were washed up on a desert island and Poll refused to speak. Nothing anyone could do could coax a word from him, until after several hours he pecked me on the ear and said, 'OK! I give up. How did you make the ship vanish like that?'

A PINCH OF SNUFF

I'm that buccaneer bold
young Ned Snuff.
Some people say I'm
too rough.
But I'm not really bad,
Just a bit of a lad,
Street-wise, dashing
and tough.

Postman: I think this letter's for you Ned. The name's a bit smudged.

Ned Snuff: Can't be for me then. You know my name's Ned Snuff!

Did you hear about the time Ned Snuff was sent to jail for stealing a calendar?

He got twelve months!

What did Ned Snuff do after he fell from the crow's nest?

Limp!

Yo Ho Ho

Ned Snuff: Why do I get a stabbing pain in my eye when I drink a mug of Sam's tea?

Cutlass Kate: Ever thought about taking the spoon out of the mug?

Why was Ned Snuff so scared when the *Mad Maggot* crossed the Equator?
Because he'd heard it was an imaginary lion running round the world.

When Ned Snuff is in the crow's nest, what is the farthest he can see on a sunny day? The sun!

What did Ned Snuff get when he jumped overboard? *Wet!*

Why does Ned Snuff always have a bar of soap tied around his neck?

So that if he is shipwrecked, he can wash himself ashore!

What's got a wooden leg and goes Yo-ho-ho – plop?

A pirate laughing his head off!

Who wears the biggest boots on the *Mad Maggot*?

The pirate with the biggest feet!

What did the first cannon say to the second cannon?

You're fired!

What do you get hanging from the yardarm?

Long arms!

What game was Ned Snuff wanting to play when he asked everyone on board the *Mad Maggot* to join him in the crow's nest?

Squash!

When is the Mad Maggot like a snow storm?

When it's adrift!

Did you hear about the day Ned Snuff said he felt like a pair of curtains?

Captain Blunder told him to pull himself together!

YoHoHo

Ned Snuff: I'm homesick.

Betty Bilge: But the Mad Maggot is your home now.

Ned Snuff: I know, and I'm sick of it!

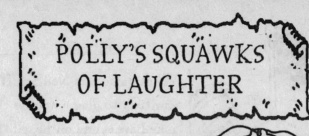

POLLY'S SQUAWKS OF LAUGHTER

How do we know that parrots are smarter than chickens?

Ever heard of Kentucky Fried Parrot?

Where do parrots go when they die?

They always get into Heaven because they're God's favourite screechers!

What do birds use when they jump out of aeroplanes?

Sparrowchutes!

What do you get if you cross a budgie with a packet of puff pastry?

Tweetie Pie!

What do birds drink first thing in the morning?

Nest-cafe!

One day I had a funny turn,
My feathers went quite wavy.
I flew away,
One day in May,
And tried to join the navy!

What do you get if you cross a budgie with a bulldog?

A budgerigrrrrr!

Ben Blunder: Eat your seed, Poll. It's good for growing parrots.

Poll: So who wants to grow parrots?

How does a parrot talk to its friends?

In pollysyllables!

Where do parrots learn to talk?
At the local polly-technic!

Yo Ho Ho

A piratical parrot called Polly,
Fell in love with an owl called Solly.
She thought, 'What the heck?'
And gave him a peck.
Now Solly thinks Polly's quite dolly.

What happened to the budgie who flew into the blender?
Shredded Tweat!

What do parrots like to watch on television?
The Feather Forecast!

What goes 'Squawk!', 'Squawk!', Bang!
A parrot walking through a minefield!

Why did the blind seagull cross the road?
To get to the birds' eye shop!

What would you get if you crossed Polly
the Parrot with Sydney the Seagull?
*A bird that asks its way home when it
gets lost!*

What do you call
a woodpecker
with no beak?
A head banger!

Knock! Knock!
Who's there?
Polly!
Polly who?
(Silence)
I said Polly who?
(Still silence)
Oh, you must be polygon!

CUTLASS KATE'S CUTTING WIT

How did Kate make a Venetian blind?
She stuck her finger in his eye!

And how did she make a Maltese cross?
She trod on his toe!

Captain Blunder: Kate! The *Hornet's* signalling us to tell them our position.

Cutlass Kate: Tell him we're just good friends, but I'm working on it!

Cutlass Kate: Cap'n! Betty Bilge has volunteered to sail with Bill Sharkie for a voyage to the Caribbean.

Ben Blunder: Jamaica?

Cutlass Kate: Don't you listen. I said she volunteered!

Why was Cutlass Kate worried when she saw two elephants on a beach?

She was afraid they might drop their trunks!

Ben Blunder: Kate! Call me a sedan chair.

Cutlass Kate: If you insist, but you'll still be Ben Blunder to me, Sedan.

Ned Snuff: Can you telephone from the *Mad Maggot*?

Cutlass Kate: Of course, any fool can tell a phone from the *Mad Maggot*.

Captain Blunder: During a skirmish one day, I fell overboard and was swallowed by a whale.

Cutlass Kate: How did you escape?

Captain Blunder: It set me free because it couldn't stomach me.

What did Roger Jolly do when he caught Cutlass Kate stealing rhubarb?
He put her in custardy!

Cutlass Kate: I have a stuffed tiger at home that reminds me of my uncle.

Captain Blunder: What's he stuffed with?

Cutlass Kate: My uncle!

Ned Snuff: Kate, watch me swing from the crow's nest!

Cutlass Kate: If you fall and break your legs, don't come running to me!

Cutlass Kate:	Oh Doctor, thank goodness you're here! Cap'n Blunder's broken a leg.
Doctor:	But I'm a doctor of music.
Cutlass Kate:	That's fine, it's the piano leg.

Hairdresser:	How would you like your hair, Madam?
Cutlass Kate:	Could you make it look like a straggly haystack?
Hairdresser:	I couldn't possibly bring myself to do that to you, Madam.
Cutlass Kate:	Why not? That's what you did last time I was here!

Yo Ho Ho

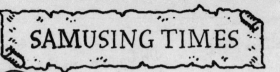

Sam eats peas with honey.
He's done it all his life.
It makes the peas taste funny.
But keeps them on his knife!

How did Sweaty Sam make
an apple crumble?
He hit it with a hammer!

And how did he make an apple puff?
He chased it round the galley!

Sweaty Sam: I've got frog's legs, Cap'n.
Captain Blunder: Hop off, Sam!

Captain Blunder: Sam! You've got your thumb
in my soup.
Sweaty Sam: It's all right, Cap'n. It's not
hot.

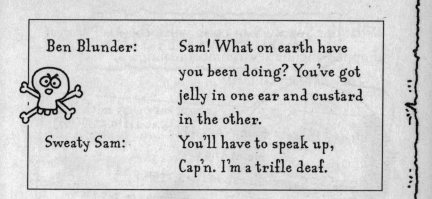

| Ben Blunder: | Sam! What on earth have you been doing? You've got jelly in one ear and custard in the other. |
| Sweaty Sam: | You'll have to speak up, Cap'n. I'm a trifle deaf. |

What did Sweaty Sam's right eye say to his left eye?
Between you and me, something smells.

Ben Blunder:	How did you break your tooth, Ned?
Ned Snuff:	On Sweaty Sam's tomato sauce.
Ben Blunder:	But tomatoes are soft.
Ned Snuff:	Not when they're still in their cans, they're not!

As a cook, Sweaty Sam was disgusting.
His pans and his pots were all rusting.
His mince was too runny,
His cakes tasted funny,
And his stews were simply gut busting.

What did Sweaty Sam cook when the *Mad Maggot* dropped anchor at a cannibal island?

Human beans on toast!

Betty Bilge: Sam, your apple soufflé reminds me of the sea.

Sweaty Sam: Because it's green and frothy?

Betty Bilge: No. Because it makes me sick!

Captain Blunder: Sam, why have you got your thumb on my steak?

Sweaty Sam: So it doesn't fall off the plate again.

Sweaty Sam: How did you find the steak, Cap'n?

Captain Blunder: I moved a pea and guess what! There it was.

Yo Ho Ho

Captain Blunder: Sam, there are flies on my soup.

Sweaty Sam: Would you prefer soup on your flies, Cap'n?

Ben Blunder: I'm feeling really hungry today, Sam. What do you recommend?

Sweaty Sam: Dinner in the Legge Arms, Sir.

Captain Blunder: Sam, I want a glass of water and some fish for lunch.

Sweaty Sam: Fillet, Cap'n?

Captain Blunder: Yes! Right up to the top.

Captain Blunder: Sam, there are two flies playing football in my soup.

Sweaty Sam: They're practising for the Cup Final tomorrow.

Cutlass Kate: Sam, this soup tastes funny.

Sweaty Sam: So how come no one's laughing?

ON WITH THE MOTLEY

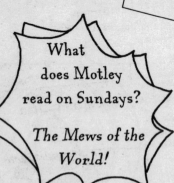

What did the three-legged cat who went into a Wild West saloon say?

'I'm looking for my paw!'

Yo Ho Ho

What does Motley the Cat have for breakfast?

Mice Crispies!

How could Beastly Bill Sharkie tell that Motley had a bad cold?

He had really bad cat-arrh!

What does Motley read on Sundays?

The Mews of the World!

Why does Motley chase birds?

Just for a lark!

What did Motley do after he ate a pound of cheese?

Went mousing with baited breath!

Why did Nasty Norman cover Motley in egg white and bake him in a slow oven?

He wanted a catameringue!

How did Beastly Bill Sharkie know that Motley had eaten a duck?

He had that down in the mouth look!

Why are some cats longer in the evening than they are during the day?

Because they're taken out in the evening and taken in in the morning!

What do you call a cat that hangs out with the gang?
A posse!

What would you get if you crossed Motley the Cat with a roast duck?
A duck-filled fatty-puss!

What do you get if you cross Motley with a woodpile?
Catalogues!

How does Motley eat lasagne?
He puts it in his mouth like everyone else!

Yo Ho Ho

Where does Motley buy his furniture?
Habicat!

What's Motley's favourite French pudding?
Chocolate mousse!

What did the little boy say when he saw Motley in a chemist shop?

'Look, Mum. Puss in Boots!'

What do you get if you cross Motley with a lemon?

A sourpuss!

How much does Motley pay for his cat food?

Twenty pence purr can!

What would you get if you crossed Motley with a Pekingese?

A Peking Tom!

A JOLLY FUNNY TIME

One Christmas, Lieutenant R. Jolly,
Sat on a huge bunch of holly.
Gosh, did he jump!
Then he fell on his rump,
And everyone laughed at the wally.

What did Roger Jolly do when a seven foot tall pirate escaped from the *Hornet's* hold along with a five foot tall buccaneer?
He looked high and low for them!

What did an X-ray of Roger Jolly's brain show he had?
Not a lot!

Which underwater rogue is Roger Jolly keen to capture?

Jack the Kipper!

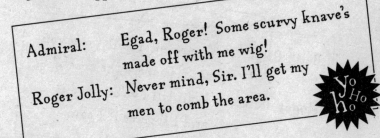

Admiral: Egad, Roger! Some scurvy knave's made off with me wig!

Roger Jolly: Never mind, Sir. I'll get my men to comb the area.

Where did Roger Jolly challenge Captain Blunder to a sword fight?

On a dual carriageway!

Roger Jolly: Captain Ben Blunder, I arrest you in the name of the king.

Ben Blunder: What's the charge?

Roger Jolly: There's no charge – it's quite free!

What was Roger Jolly doing up a tree, peering at the *Mad Maggot* through his telescope?

He was working for the Special Branch!

Why did Sydney the Seagull put a loaf of bread in Roger Jolly's favourite comic?
Because he knew Roger liked crumby jokes!

Yo Ho Ho

Betty Bilge: Commander Jolly, can you see me across the creek?

Roger Jolly: Wait till I've crossed it and I'll wave if I can.

When do the crew of the *Hornet* have their main meal of the day?
At launch time!

On one voyage, why was the *Hornet* full of bones?
Because Roger Jolly could only raise a skeleton crew!

What happened when Roger Jolly's diary got washed overboard?
It was water-logged!

Why was the wench who Roger Jolly rescued from the clutches of Ned Sharkie, purple with anger?

She was a damson in distress!

Roger Jolly: You there! You'll need a permit to fish from the quay.

Sailor: No thanks, I'm doing fine with a worm.

Roger Jolly: When my father retired from the navy, his men gave him an illuminated address.

Sailor: How did they do that?

Roger Jolly: They set fire to his house!

What did Roger Jolly do when he heard he stood a good chance of catching Captain Blunder if he sailed in a cutter?

He bought himself a sea-saw!

What did Roger Jolly call the sailor
who could float on water?

Bob!

What did Roger Jolly call the sailor
who drove a truck to work?

Laurie!

Sailor: I'm too tired to scrub the
deck, Sir.

Roger Jolly: Don't be silly. Hard work
never harmed anyone.

Sailor: So why should I risk
being first?

What happened to the sailors who abandoned ship and ran away with the circus?

Roger Jolly made them bring it back!

Yo Ho Ho

Why did Roger Jolly enter the Hornet's crew in the Legge Arms' football tournament?

Just for kicks!

Roger Jolly: I hope I didn't see your men attacking that English galleon, Ben Blunder.

Ben Blunder: I hope you didn't see them either...

Why did the Little Mermaid blush?

Because she saw the Hornet's bottom!

Sydney Seagull's in the sky,
Making messes from on high.
Roger Jolly's wipes his eye.
Thanking God that pigs don't fly!

Why was the black
and white seabird
always panting?
It was a puffin!

On which side does
a seagull have most
feathers?
On the outside!

46

What do you call a ten metre tall, angry seagull with a potato in its ear?

Anything you want. It can't hear you!

What do you get if you cross a seagull with a cement mixer?

I don't know, but if you see one flying overhead, get out the way quickly!

Why does Sydney believe everything you tell him?

Because he's such a gullible bird!

What do you call a seagull armed with a machine gun?

Sir!

Two seagulls were circling over a cliff one day when Concorde flew overhead. 'Golly,' said one. 'I wish I could fly as fast as that.' 'You could,' said the the other. 'If your bum was on fire.'

Why is a well–fed seagull like a plump sofa?
Because they're both well stuffed!

What's a young seagull on the eve of its first birthday?
364 days old!

When did Sydney start to think he was a banjo?
The day that Roger Jolly started to pick on him!

Yo Ho Ho

What do you call a seagull that lays concrete eggs?
A brick-layer!

And where does he meet his mate for a drink?
In a crow bar!

Sydney: Roger Jolly plays the piano by ear.

Poll: So what? Cap'n Blunder fiddles with his whiskers!

A LOAD OF OLD BILGE

('Less of the 'old', pleeeeease!')

One night while anchored off Dover,
Betty Bilge knitted Ben a pullover.
But would you believe,
She knitted four sleeves?
And now it only fits Rover!

Why did Betty take a fancy to the Legge Arms' caretaker?

Because he swept her off her feet!

Ben Blunder: Betty Bilge, stop fighting with Kate. Learn a bit of give and take.

Betty Bilge: I have, Cap'n. She took my brooch, so I gave her a black eye.

Betty Bilge: How do you keep an idiot in suspense.

Ben Blunder: I don't know.

Betty Bilge: I'll tell you later.

(Haven't we had this joke before? Ed. Silence, Dog!)

Yo Ho Ho

Betty Bilge: Before I became a pirate, I thought about working in a bank.

Captain Blunder: Whatever for?

Betty Bilge: Because I heard there was lots of money in it!

What do you call a rowing boat in the middle of the ocean?

Lost!

Roger Jolly: Have you been a pirate all your life?

Betty Bilge: Not yet!

Cutlass Kate: I heard a new joke yesterday. Did I tell it to you?

Betty Bilge: Was it funny?

Cutlass Kate: Hilarious!

Betty Bilge: Then you didn't tell it to me!

How did Viking pirates contact each other at sea?

They used Norse Code!

Betty Bilge: Do you want to sail with us to France?

Sailor: Oui! Oui!

Betty Bilge: Well be quick. We sail in five minutes.

Which Italian pirates beat up people with shopping baskets?

The Rafia!

Why was Betty reluctant to sail to the west coast of South America?

Chile made her fart! (Sorry: break wind.)

Betty Bilge:	The doctor's given me this cream for my spots.
Cutlass Kate:	Did he say it would definitely work?
Betty Bilge:	No! He wouldn't make rash promises.

'New pair of breeches, please,' Betty Bilge said to the shop assistant.

'Of courth, Madam,' lisped the assistant. 'Walk this way.'

'I'm not sure I want them that tight!' said Betty.

Why was Betty Bilge wearing flat-heeled boots?
Because her high-heeled ones were at the cobblers!

Betty Bilge: Oh Cap'n, I feel like a bridge!
Ben Blunder: What's come over you?
Betty Bilge: Three sedan chairs and a herd of cows.

Why did the *Mad Maggot's* cleaner quit her job?
Because she found grime didn't pay!

Yo Ho Ho

What sits at the bottom of the ocean and spends all its time weeping?
A nervous wreck!

How do pirates get from one ship to another?
Taxi crab!

PLUMBING THE DEPTHS

Who's the most famous gangster in the sea? *Al Caprawn!*

What do mermaids eat for breakfast? *Toast and mermalade!*

What's the most musical fish in the sea? *The piano tuna!*

What sort of fish do dead pirates eat? *Angel fish!*

Who are the worst thieves in the sea? *Crabs — because they're always pinching things!*

Yo Ho Ho

What do dead fish use to help them hear? *Herring aids!*

What watery creature is always saying 'yes'? *The seal of approval!*

What kind of fish tries to lend you money? *A loan shark!*

Yo Ho Ho

What did the pirate say when he saw the giant octopus? *Look out! He's heavily armed!*

Did you hear about the nudist fish? *They went around shark naked!*

What part of a fish weighs most? *The scales!*

How do you stop fish from smelling? *Bung something up their noses!*

What's a shark's favourite game? *Swallow My Leader!*

Where do down-and-out fish live? *On Squid Row!*

Where do whales go to be weighed? *The whale-weigh station!*

Where do fish go to raise money? *The prawnbroker!*

What do you get if you cross a salmon with a one room apartment? *A little flatfish!*

Yo Ho Ho

What's the best way to get a message to a mackerel? *Drop it a line!*

What's the best way to catch a fish? *Get a friend to throw one at you!*

What do you get if you cross a shark with a snowball? *Frostbite!*

What sea creature sits on London's South Bank and spends its time going round and round? *The Millennium Whale!*

What's the best way to talk to a man-eating shark? *Long distance!*

Why did the shark cross the ocean? *To get to the other tide!*

What fish cares for sick pets? *The veterinary sturgeon!*

yo Ho ho

Which is the most musical fish in the sea, man? *The rock salmon!*

What dance do eels enjoy at parties? *The Conger!*

Do sea mammals enjoy life? *Enjoy it? They have a whale of a time!*

What did the angler say to his girlfriend when they hooked the same fish? *'Your plaice or mine?'*

What sleeps at the bottom of the ocean *A kipper!*

SHARKIE'S SHRIEKERS

Why did Beastly Bill Sharkie's breeches fall down? *He forgot to splice his mainbraces!*

Yo Ho Ho

When the crew of the *Vulture* were on a voyage to the Far East, they discovered an island where the natives ate something that was a cross between a roll of Sellotape and peanut butter. *It didn't taste of much, but it sure as heck stuck to the roof of your mouth!*

Which friend of Beastly Bill Sharkie has the number '3' painted on his chest and 'To Terminus' on his head? *Captain Blunder-bus!*

What film made Beastly Bill Sharkie a film star? *Jawsie!*

Beastly Bill Sharkie's first mate, Nasty Norman, was eating a bacon sarnie outside the Legge Arms one day when a woman with a small yappy dog sat down at the next table. The dog pestered Norman for some of his sandwich. 'Can I throw him a bit?' Norman asked the woman.

'How kind,' she said. 'Of course you can.'

So Norman bent down, picked up the dog and threw it over the wall!

What did the grape say when Beastly Bill Sharkie trod on it?

Nothing, it just gave out a little whine!

When the *Vulture* was overrun with rats, Beastly Bill Sharkie went to a shop and asked for rat poison.

'We don't stock it,' said the shopkeeper. 'Have you tried Boots?'

'Look. I want to poison them,' said Sharkie, 'not kick them to death!'

Why did the *Vulture's* carpenter break all his teeth?
He couldn't stop biting his nails!

'Cap'n Sharkie, I don't want to go to the Spice Islands!'
'Shut up, Norman, and keep swimming or I'll puncture your arm bands!'

What's the difference between Beastly Bill Sharkie and a packet of crisps?
People like crisps!

Why does Beastly Bill Sharkie never get seasick?
Because he bolts his food down!

Why did Beastly Bill Sharkie carry an axe?

He had a splitting headache!

What did Nasty Norman say when Beastly Bill Sharkie threatened to give him a taste of the cat o'nine tails?

Mee-ow-ow-ow-ow-ow-ow-ow-ow-ow!

Did you hear about the time the crew of the *Vulture* boarded a ship and stripped it bare of everything apart from the soap and towels?

The dirty so-and-sos!

Why did Nasty Norman grow a beard?
So no one could call him a bare-faced liar!

Yo Ho Ho

How did Beastly Bill Sharkie keep his crew on their toes?
He put drawing pins on their chairs!

Beastly Bill Sharkie: Why are you crying, Norman?

Nasty Norman: My pet hamster died last night after I washed it in Persil.

Beastly Bill Sharkie: Norman! You must know that Persil's bad for hamsters.

Nasty Norman: Oh, it wasn't the Persil that killed it, Cap'n. It was the spin drier.

Beastly Bill Sharkie: Norman, why are you scratching yourself?

Nasty Norman: Because I'm the only one who knows where I itch!

Nasty Norman:	Cap'n! I've just swallowed a lightbulb.
Beastly Bill Sharkie:	Well spit it out, man. That'll de-light you.

Why did Nasty Norman swallow an Oxo cube? *Because Beastly Bill Sharkie told him it was time to take stock of himself!*

Yo Ho Ho

Nasty Norman:	I didn't know you did bird impersonations, Cap'n.
Beastly Bill Sharkie:	Me? I can't even whistle!
Nasty Norman:	No, but you watch me like a hawk.

Why did Nasty Norman aim the *Vulture's* cannon at a bowl of peas? *Because Beastly Bill Sharkie told him to shell them!*

GIRL TALK

Friends they may be, and comrades at arms too, but when Cutlass Kate and Betty Bilge, the belles of the buccaneering world, get together, things can get a little tense! Take, for example, the time Betty found Kate sobbing on the poop deck...

'Kate,' said Betty. 'Why are you crying?'

'Because Ben Blunder hit his thumb with a hammer,' sobbed Kate.

'Knowing you, I'm surprised you didn't laugh,' said Betty.

'I did,' sniffed Kate. 'That's why he hit my thumb with the hammer and that's why I'm crying.'

'Never mind,' said Betty. 'Come into my cabin and I'll put the kettle on.'

'Don't do that,' said Kate. 'I quite like the tunic you're wearing.'

o o o🐡 🐡o o o

'Whenever I'm down in the dumps, I buy myself new clothes,' said Kate.

'Oh,' said Betty. 'I wondered where you found them!'

o o o🐡 🐡o o o

'What I'd really like,' said Kate, 'is an ice cream, covered in hot chocolate sauce.'

'And a cherry on top?' suggested Betty.

'Don't be silly,' scoffed Kate. 'I'm on a diet.'

'I've just noticed that your tunic is full of holes,' said Kate, when Betty gave her a cup of tea.

Betty shrugged her shoulders. 'Couldn't give a darn,' she said.

* * *

'Talking of clothes,' Betty went on. 'I'm getting a beautiful new silk dress for the Pirates' Ball.'

'What colour?' asked Kate.

'Something to match my eyes,' said Betty.

'Oh, I didn't know they dyed silk bloodshot!'

* * *

'Cap'n Blunder said my eyes were like pools,' sighed Kate.

'Yes,' Betty nodded. 'Football pools...'

* * *

'...But you do have the face of a saint,' said Betty, smiling at Kate.

'Oh Betty, how sweet you are.' Kate purred.

'Not really,' said Betty. 'I meant a Saint Bernard!'

Betty glared at Kate. 'Your ears
smell like flowers,' she said.
    'Pink lilies?'
    'No!' Betty said. 'Cauliflowers.'

∘ ∘ ∘ 🐟 🐟 ∘ ∘ ∘

'Your teeth are like the stars, Betty,' said Kate.
    'Because they're so white and sparkling?'
    'No! Because they come out at night!'

Betty stood up and put her hands on her hips. 'Oh Betty,' said Kate. 'Your hands, they're like petals.'

'Rose petals, you mean?'

'No! Bicycle pedals.'

o o o 🐡 🐡 o o o

Kate twisted a strand of hair round a finger.

'I used to have long, wavy hair,' said Betty.

'Well, now it's waving you goodbye.'

o o o 🐡 🐡 o o o

'All this backchat is giving me a headache,' said Kate.

'Put your head through a window,' suggested Betty.

'Why?' asked Kate.

'It'll make the pane disappear!'

o o o 🐡 🐡 o o o

Just then a curious smell wafted through Betty's cabin. 'What's that?' sniffed Kate.

'Whatever Sam's cooking for dinner,' replied Betty.

'Poor Sam,' said Kate. 'You know he broke his leg tap dancing!'

'What happened?' asked Betty.

'He fell in the sink.'

'I hear he's got a skunk in his cabin!' said Betty.

'Smells awful,' said Kate.

'Yes,' Betty nodded. 'But it's getting used to the pong.'

'Did you know that Sweaty Sam does farmyard impressions?' Kate said.

'You mean he moos like a cow, and baas like a sheep?'

'No!' Kate shook her head. 'He smells!'

yo Ho ho

Kate put her cup down. 'Thanks for the tea, Betty. Better be going.'

'Going out tonight?'

'Yes,' said Kate. 'Peg-Leg Hawkins has asked me out.'

'The one-legged barman from the Legge Arms?' Betty nodded. 'He asked me out last week,' she said.

'And did you go?'

'No!' Betty shook her head. 'I told him to hop it!'

○ ○ ○ 🐡 🐡 ○ ○ ○

'Before you go Kate. I've made up a poem about you. Want to hear it?'

'That's funny,' said Betty. 'I've made up one about you too.'

'You first,' said Kate.

'OK,' said Betty, clearing her throat. 'Here goes –

That pretty young lass, Cutlass Kate,
Got a job as a pirate, first rate.
But, hook, line and sinker,
She fell for a tinker,
Now Kate's, a land-lubber's first mate.'

'I like that,' laughed Kate.
'I'll tell you mine now –

A petticoat pirate called Betty,
Was lumpy, and spotty and sweaty.
At Poole, in south Dorset,
She burst through her corset,
And banged her backside on the jetty.'

Kate and Betty laughed so loudly they almost didn't hear someone shout from above.

'That's the Cap'n, isn't it?' said Betty. 'What's he saying.'

'All hands on deck, I think,' said Kate.

'Well, he can go whistle,' said Betty. 'Last time I had my hands on deck, Sweaty Sam trod on them!'

BARKING MAD

What happened when Rover attacked a skeleton? *He left it without a leg to stand on!*

Captain Blunder: Rover is just like one of the crew.

Ned Snuff: Really? Which one?

Did you hear about the dog who ate a box of garlic? *Its bark was much worse than its bite!*

What did Rover do when his tail was accidentally cut off? *He went to a re-tail shop!*

Rover: My name's Rover. What's yours?

Dog: I'm not sure, but I think it's Fetch.

Why was Rover in the doghouse the day Captain Blunder ordered the *Mad Maggot* to be repainted?
Because the stupid mutt saw a sign saying 'WET PAINT' – so he did!

How did Captain Blunder cure Rover's habit of chasing everyone on a bicycle?
He took his bicycle away!

Where does Captain Blunder leave Rover when he goes ashore?
He ties him to a barking metre!

Did you hear about the day Dirty Dan went into a shop and at the bottom of a flight of stairs saw a sign that said, 'Dogs must be carried'?
He went back to the Mad Maggot to fetch Rover so he had a dog to carry!

Captain Blunder: Did you know that Rover plays chess?

Sharkie: I didn't know he was so smart!

Captain Blunder: He's not all that clever; I usually beat him three times out of four.

What do you get if you cross a dog with a tiger?
Very worried postmen!

Did you hear about the dog that went to the flea circus?
It stole the show!

Yo Ho Ho

What kind of dog always smells of onions?
A hot dog!

What's the yukkiest dog in the world?
A Snotweiller!

DIRTY DAN JOKES

Dan was shaving one day when the *Mad Maggot* hit a rock and juddered so much the mirror cracked along the middle. 'Britlingsea Barnacles!' gasped Dan. 'I've gone and cut my throat!'

Dan was sitting in the Legge Arms one day when Norman sidled up to him and said, 'I'll give you the winner of the Derby for five doubloons!'

'Don't be so stupidsome,' laughed Dan. 'There's just enough room in my cabin for me. Where would I keep a racehorse?'

When Dan decided to write a book about his days aboard the *Mad Maggot*, Captain Blunder suggested he write under a pen name. So he called himself Fountain!

Ben Blunder: Dan, I've fallen in love with a comely wench with a bad leg named Doris.

Dan: And what's her good leg called?

Did you hear about the wally who Dirty Dan captured and put in the *Mad Maggot's* hold?

He tried to tunnel his way out!

What did Dirty Dan do when the hand fell off his watch?

He went to get a new one in a second hand shop!

Why didn't Dirty Dan enter the Legge Arms' water polo competition?

He couldn't find a pony that could swim!

Bill Blunder: Why do you want shore leave, Dan?

Dirty Dan: To see a dentist about my wisdom teeth.

Bill Blunder: Having them taken out?

Dirty Dan: No, having them put in.

When the crew of the *Mad Maggot* boarded an Irish pirate ship, Dirty Dan found a chest full of what he thought were diamonds but which Captain Blunder could see were cut glass stones.

'Don't bother with these,' called Captain Blunder. 'They're only shamrocks!'

Dirty Dan:	I came in to get something for Betty Bilge.
Shopkeeper:	How much are you asking for her?

Dirty Dan:	I've broken my new glasses. Will I have to be examined all over again?
Optician:	No, Dan. Just your eyes.

When Captain Blunder asked Dan to repair a cannon hole on the port side of the *Mad Maggot* he was surprised an hour or two later, to see Dan throwing half the nails away. 'Why are you doing that?' he called. 'Because the heads are on the wrong end,' replied Dan.

'Fool!' cried the Captain. 'These are the nails for the other side of the ship.'

Why didn't Dirty Dan chase Norman when
Norman nicked his watch?
Because he didn't have the time!

Dirty Dan went into a shop and said to the assistant,
'May I try on those breeches in the window?'

'If you want,' said the assistant. 'But wouldn't you
feel more comfortable in the fitting room?'

Dirty Dan ran into a hardware shop. 'Quick! A
mousetrap please,' he panted. 'I've a ship to catch.'

'Sorry,' said the assistant. 'We haven't got any as
big as that.'

Dirty Dan rushed into the Legge Arms one day,
asked for a glass of water, ran out with it and came
back a second or two later asking for the empty glass
to be refilled as quickly as possible.

'You must be thirsty!' said the barmaid.

'I'm not drinking it,' Dan gasped. 'The *Mad
Maggot's* on fire!'

Why did Dirty Dan start staring at ink blotters all day?

He found it an absorbing hobby.

Captain Blunder: Any luck fishing, Dan?
Dirty Dan: Yes, Cap'n. We caught three cod and a potfor.
Captain Blunder: What's a potfor?
Dirty Dan: To cook the cod in, Sir.

Captain Blunder: Why did you leave your last ship, Dan?
Dirty Dan: Illness, Cap'n.
Captain Blunder: Serious?
Dirty Dan: Not really, the captain got sick of me.

What did Dirty Dan call the man he saw wearing a raincoat?
Mac!

And what did he call the man he saw wearing two raincoats?
Max!

Why did Dirty Dan never swim on an empty stomach?
Because it's easier to swim in water!

Dirty Dan:	Have you heard the gossip about the butter?
Cutlass Kate:	No!
Dirty Dan:	Better not tell you, you'll just spread it.

Captain Blunder:	Dan! Why did dreaming about football make you late for the middle watch?
Dirty Dan:	Because they were playing extra time!

A word of advice from Dirty Dan:

Don't eat Sweaty Sam's dinners,
Better to throw them aside.
A lot of men didn't,
And a lot of men died.
The meat's tough as iron.
The veg made of steel.
And if they don't kill you,
The puddings sure will!

ROUND THE CLOCK LAUGHTER

Midnight

Ned Snuff took over from Dirty Dan on watch. The two chatted for a while before Dan decided to turn in for the night. 'How long after midnight is it now?' asked Dan.

'Dunno!' said Ned. 'My watch only goes as high as twelve!'

1.00am

 Unable to sleep, Captain Ben Blunder went on deck and as he was talking to Dirty Dan a clock on shore struck one. 'Doesn't that clock get on your nerves, ringing every quarter of an hour?' Ben Blunder asked Dan.

'Sure as a barnacle breaches a trundlesome Tawsole,' said Dan. 'I've often thought about rowing ashore and smashing it, but I don't want to be charged with killing time.'

2.00am

Down below, Sweaty Sam's snoring was so loud, it woke up Betty Bilge who was in the next cabin. 'Sam!' she cried, knocking on the wall. 'Do you always snore?'

'No!' yawned Sam, sitting up in bed and scratching his armpits, 'Only when I'm asleep.'

3.00am

Not able to get back to sleep after Betty Bilge had woken him, Sam decided to go to the galley and make an early start on the breakfast. 'Think I'll make some doughnuts,' he thought, then changed his mind as he was sick of the hole business.

4.00am _____

Not far away, aboard the *Vulture*, Nasty Norman and
Beastly Bill Sharkie were plotting how to steal a
treasure map from Ben Blunder when the full moon
came from under a cloud and lit up the ship. 'I
wonder,' said Nasty Norman, 'which is heavier, a
full moon or a half moon.'

'Ignorant dog,' boomed Bill Sharkie. ''Tis perfectly
obvious a half moon is heavier.'

'Why?' asked Norman.

'Because a full moon is twice as light.'

5.00am _____

Dawn. There was a knock on Cutlass Kate's cabin
door. 'Come in,' Kate called brightly. Sam put his
head round the door to tell Kate breakfast was ready
and saw her sitting up in her cabin staring through
her porthole. 'I love this cabin,' Kate said. 'I can lie
in my hammock and watch the sun rise.'

'So what,' said Sweaty Sam. 'I can sit at the
breakfast table and watch the kitchen sink!'

6.00am _____

'Sam!' cried Captain Blunder. 'This bacon tastes
awful.'

'I've been cooking bacon since before you were born,' grumbled Sweaty Sam.

'Maybe,' said Ben Blunder. 'But why did you have to save it for me?'

7.00am

'On deck, everyone,' ordered Captain Blunder. 'You're all about as fit as a fat flea with a broken foot. Exercise time.'

The crew of the *Mad Maggot* grumbled as they made their way out of the galley. 'Now,' boomed Ben Blunder, 'on your backs and circle your feet in the air as though you're bicycling. Sam! Move your feet! Pretend you're on a bike.'

'I am,' moaned Sam. 'I'm free-wheeling!'

8.00am

'I say, my Man,' said Roger Jolly to one of his sailors. 'Have you swabbed the decks and emptied the bilges?'

'Aye, aye, Sir,' said the sailor. 'And I've swept the horizon with your telescope.'

9.00am

'What are you doing, Dan?' Captain Blunder asked

Dirty Dan when he found him sawing the legs off his bed.

'Roger Jolly saw me board a merchantman and I thought I'd better lie low for a while.'

10.00am ————————————————————

'Coffee?' Cutlass Kate asked Betty Bilge.

'No thanks,' said Betty. 'I don't feel at all perky!'

11.00am ————————————————————

Captain Blunder came on deck, clutching his stomach. 'What's the matter?' asked Cutlass Kate.

'Acid indigestion,' gasped Ben Blunder. 'Don't know what to do for it!'

'You could stop drinking acid!'

Noon

'I hear Roger Jolly wants to be higher than an admiral,' said Ben Blunder to Bill Sharkie.

'Nothing's higher than an admiral, surely,' said Bill Sharkie.

'Something is,' said Ned Snuff who had overheard.

'What's that?' both captains asked.

'His hat!'

1.00pm

'Sam, there's a dead fly in my soup,' said Captain Blunder at lunchtime.

'What do you expect on the money you give me,' said Sam. 'A live one?'

2.00pm

Captain Blunder went ashore to do some shopping and on the way back went into a cafe for a coffee.

'Five doubloons please,' said the waiter.

Ben Blunder gave the waiter the money.

'We don't get many pirates in here,' said the waiter, pocketing the gold coins.

'I'm not surprised,' said Captain Blunder. 'With coffee at five doubloons a cup!'

——————————————————

'There's a smoke signal coming from that hill over there,' Ned Snuff shouted down from the crow's-nest.

'What's the matter?' Ben Blunder called back.

'The people sending it have no water!' came the reply.

'Are they praying for rain?' Ben Blunder wanted to know.

'No,' shouted Ned. 'They're calling for the plumber!'

4.00pm ——————————————————————————

'I've put the kettle on,' Betty Bilge said at teatime.

'So I see,' said Captain Blunder.

'Wouldn't a hat have been better?'

5.00pm ——————————————————————————

'Next!' called Captain Blunder to the line of would-be pirates wanting to join the *Mad Maggot*.

'Me, Sir,' a weedy little man stepped forward.

'What're your qualifications?' Ben asked.

'I'm a reformed pickpocket!' the man replied.

'And what do you do now?'

'Well, sir,' said the man. 'I walk into shops and put things in peoples' pockets!'

6.00pm

'Captain,' panted Ned Snuff who had been ashore. 'I've just heard that Roger Jolly's feeding dynamite to some hens.'

'What's he doing that for?' wondered Ben Blunder.

'He wanted some mine layers!'

7.00pm

Dirty Dan came aboard, a wide smile on his face.

'What are you so pleased about?' asked Betty Bilge.

'Roger Jolly's ordered the gallows to be taken down,' grinned Dan. 'And no noose is good noose!'

8.00pm

'Sam!' yelled Captain Blunder at supper. 'This stew isn't fit for a pig.'

'Hang on,' said Sam. 'I'll bring you some that is!'

9.00pm

'Think I'll turn in early and finish my book,' said Cutlass Kate.

'What are you reading?' asked Betty Bilge.

'*All You Need to Know About Gunpowder* by Dinah Mite!'

10.00pm ──────────────────────────

'I can't wait to go to bed tonight,' yawned Betty
Bilge. 'I've got a new one.'

'Spring mattress?' asked Dirty Dan.

'No!' said Betty. 'An all-year-round one.'

11.00pm ──────────────────────────

'That planet over there's Mars!' said Dirty
Dan pointing up at the sky.

'Really,' said Ned Snuff. 'Which
one's Pa's then?'

Midnight ──────────────────────────

Ned Snuff took over from Dirty Dan on watch...

Have a good giggle with the other joke books
in this series. They're sometimes wacky,
often silly but always worth sharing!

And delve into the diaries!
Follow the daily shenanigans in the lives of
the Gory vampire family, pirate Captain Ben
Blunder and alien traveller Zorb Zork and their
friends. Then bone-up on vampires, pirates and
aliens in the fascinating Spotters Guides.

But make sure you don't miss vampires,
pirates and aliens on your televisions!